The
four friends
and other stories

Nelson

Thomas Nelson and Sons Ltd
Nelson House   Mayfield Road
Walton-on-Thames   Surrey
KT12 5PL   UK

51 York Place
Edinburgh
EH1 3JD   UK

Thomas Nelson (Hong Kong) Ltd
Toppan Building 10/F
22A Westlands Road
Quarry Bay   Hong Kong

Thomas Nelson Australia
102 Dodds Street
South Melbourne
Victoria 3205   Australia

Nelson Canada
1120 Birchmount Road
Scarborough   Ontario
M1K 5G4   Canada

© Macmillan Education Ltd 1987
This edition © Thomas Nelson & Sons Ltd 1992
Editorial Consultant: Donna Bailey
'The four friends' was written by Donna Bailey and illustrated by Francis Scholes
'The lost seagull' was written by Penny Hegarty and illustrated by Ursula Sieger
'Honey for tea' was written by Donna Bailey and illustrated by David Dowland
and Joyce Smith

First published by Macmillan Education Ltd 1987
ISBN 0-333-41887-5

This edition published by Thomas Nelson and Sons Ltd 1992

ISBN 0-17-400615-2
NPN 9 8 7 6 5

Printed in Hong Kong

The four friends

    Once upon a time there were four friends.
They lived on a farm and worked hard
for the farmer.
The donkey helped the farmer carry
sacks of corn.
The dog kept the robbers away.
The cat caught the mice in the barn and
the cock looked after all the hens
in the farmyard.

One day the friends heard the farmer say to his wife, "I must get rid of that old donkey. He is too slow and old."

The farmer's wife said, "I must get rid of that cat. He is too fat and too old to catch the mice."

Then the farmer said, "That dog lies all day in the sun. He is getting too old and blind, and I think we should eat that old cock for dinner on Sunday."

The four friends were very unhappy when they heard what the farmer and his wife said.

"We must run away," said the donkey.

"We must go today," said the dog.

"We shall find a new home," said the cat.

"And I will not be the farmer's Sunday dinner," said the cock.

So that night the four friends left the farm.
They walked and walked down the road until
they came to a dark wood.

"I am getting tired," said the dog.

"And I am very hungry," said the cat.

"We must find somewhere to stay,"
said the donkey.

"Look, I can see a light over there,"
said the cock, who was sitting on
the donkey's back.

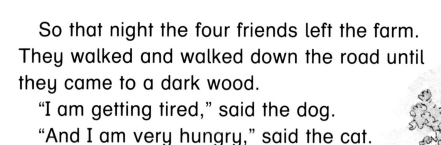

Through the trees in the wood, they saw
a cottage with a light in the window.

"Let's see who lives here," said the donkey.
So as he was the tallest, he went up to
the window and looked in.

"What can you see?" asked the dog.

"I can see a table spread with good food and
drink and there are three robbers sitting at
the table," said the donkey.

"That would just suit us," said the cock.

"Yes, if only we were in there,"
said the donkey.

The four friends began to think of how
they could drive the robbers out.
At last they thought of a plan.
The donkey put his front feet on
the window ledge.
The dog jumped on the donkey's back.
The cat climbed on top of the dog.
The cock flew up and sat on the cat's head.
Then all together they began to make
as much noise as they could.

The donkey brayed, the dog barked,
the cat mewed and the cock crowed.

The robbers were very frightened by
this noise.
They saw a strange monster looking in
the window, so they ran out of the cottage
as fast as their legs would carry them.
The four friends laughed and
went into the cottage.

They sat down at the table and
had a good meal.
When they had finished, they put out
the lights and settled down to sleep.
The donkey lay down outside the back door.
The dog lay beside the door.
The cat lay on the hearth near the fire and
the cock flew up onto a cupboard.
Soon all except the cat were fast asleep.

Later that night, the robbers saw
there was no light in the cottage and
everything was quiet.

The robber chief said to one of his men,
"Go back and make sure the cottage is empty."

So the robber crept up to the cottage and
looked in through the window.
Everything was quiet, so he went into
the kitchen to light a candle.

He crept over to the fire and held the candle
close to the live coals.
But they were not live coals after all!
They were the cat's eyes glowing
in the dark and the cat jumped up,
spitting and scratching.
The cat scratched the man's face and
the man jumped up in fright.

He tried to run out of the back door but
he fell over the dog who was lying there.
The dog jumped up and bit him in the leg.
The man ran into the yard and ran into
the donkey who gave him a big kick
with his back legs.
This noise woke the cock who felt
quite fresh and awake and sang out loudly,
"Cock-a-doodle-doo!"
The robber was so frightened that
he ran back to his chief as fast as he could.

He said, "There is a horrible witch in the house who breathed on me and scratched me with her long fingers.
Behind the door stands a man with a knife who stabbed me in the leg.
In the yard is a black monster who hit me with a club, and on the roof sits a judge who called out 'Catch the robbers!'
So I ran away as fast as I could."

From that day on, the robbers dared not go near the cottage and the four friends lived in the cottage happily ever after.

The lost seagull

Stanley was a seagull.
He was a very young seagull and
he wanted an adventure.
He was bored with flying over the sea and
living on the cliffs, so one day
he spread his wings and flew over the land.
He flew a long way until he was tired,
then he landed in a field.

"Where am I?" said Stanley.
"I wish my brothers were here. I am lonely."
   He walked a little way but
the green grass tickled his feet and
the wind blew his feathers.
Suddenly a big brown furry monster
rushed at him.
Stanley was afraid and flew up into the air.
   "Oh dear," said Stanley. "I wish I could find
the sea. I am lost. What am I going to do?"

He spread his wings and flew up high.
The sun was shining and the sky was blue but
Stanley didn't care.
He wanted to go home but
he couldn't see the sea.
On and on he flew. He looked and looked but
he couldn't find his brothers or the sea.
    Then suddenly he saw it.
Down, down, down, a long way down, he saw
the sea shining brightly below him.
    "There it is!" cried Stanley.
"Now I'll find my brothers too."

He flew down as fast as he could
to the deep cold water.

"Quack, quack," said the duck. "Who are you?"

"I'm Stanley," said Stanley.
"Have you seen my brothers anywhere?"

"No," said the duck crossly.
"What sort of bird are you?"

"I'm a seagull," said Stanley.
"Haven't you seen a seagull before?"

"No," said the duck crossly. "Get off
my pond. I don't want seagulls on my pond."

"Isn't this the sea?" cried Stanley.

"No it isn't," said the duck.
"It's a pond. It's my pond and
I don't want silly seagulls on it."

Poor Stanley was very sad.
If this wasn't the sea, he would have to
go on looking for it.

"Do you know where I can find the sea?"
he asked.

"No I don't," said the duck. "Why don't you
ask that big crow over there? He might know."

"Thank you," said Stanley and he spread his
wings and flew across the field.

"Can you help me please?" said Stanley to the crow.

"I'll help you if I can," said the crow. "What do you want?"

Stanley told him he couldn't find the sea.

"Oh the sea is a long way from here," said the crow. "You'll never find it on your own."

Stanley tried hard not to cry. "I'm lost," he said. "I've lost my brothers as well."

"Come home with me," said the crow. "I'll look after you."

So Stanley flew off with the big black crow.
They flew over the fields and the houses.
At last they came to a very tall tree.

"Here we are," said the crow.
"This is my home."

"Do you live in a tree?" asked Stanley
in surprise.

The crow laughed. "You don't know very much,
do you?" he said.

"Don't you fall out of the tree in
the night?" said Stanley. He looked down.
It looked a long way down to the ground.

"No," said the crow. "Come on.
Get into the nest."

Stanley tried to get into the nest but
the nest was too small.
If Stanley sat in it, there was
no room for the crow.
If the crow sat in it, there was
no room for Stanley.

"Oh dear," said the crow. "This is no good.
You'll have to find another home."

"Yes," said Stanley sadly. "Thank you
for helping me, Crow."

So Stanley set off again.

"Where can I go now?" he said.

"I wish I could find my brothers."

It would soon be dark and he had
nowhere to go for the night.

His wings were very tired.

He would have to stop and rest.

So he flew down and sat on the roof of a barn.

"You woke me up," said an owl through
a hole in the roof.

"Oh dear," said Stanley. "I am very sorry."
Then he told fhe owl that he was lost.

"I'll tell you what to do," said the owl.
"Now listen to me. You must fly to the top
of a very tall tower. Your brothers will see
you up there when they come to look for you."

"Oh yes. I'll do that," said Stanley.
"Thank you for your help, Owl."

So Stanley flew on until he saw
a very tall tower.
He flew down and sat at the very top.
Then he waited.
He waited for a long, long time.
It was nearly dark, but he still waited.

Then suddenly he saw his brothers.
They were coming nearer and nearer.
He could hear their wings.

"Here I am!" he shouted. "Here I am!"
The big white birds flew nearer.

"There he is!" cried one of the seagulls.
"There's Stanley! Come on Stanley,
where have you been?"

Stanley laughed, then he spread his wings and
flew home with them, back to the sea.

Honey for tea

Sam was always asking questions.
"Where does the rain come from, Mum?
How do the flowers grow?
Why do cats have long whiskers?"
One day he was in the garden.
"How do bees make honey, Mum?" he asked.
"Why don't you find out?" said his Mum.
"Watch them and you will see."

"Won't the bees sting me, Mum?" asked Sam.

"Only if you make them cross," Mum said.
"Look. Follow that bee over there and
see what he does.
Don't touch him or you will frighten him."

So Sam watched the bee.
It was crawling over a big red rose.
It had pollen all over its back legs.

First the bee flew onto the apple tree.
It settled on a flower.

"Oh good," said Mum. "The bee will help
make the apples grow later on."

"How does it do that, Mum?" said Sam.

"It leaves some pollen on the flower,"
Mum said, "and later that helps
to make the fruit."

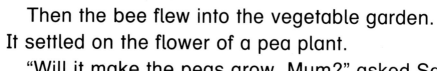

Then the bee flew into the vegetable garden.
It settled on the flower of a pea plant.

"Will it make the peas grow, Mum?" asked Sam.

"Yes," Mum said. "Later on we'll be able to
eat nice green peas now that the bee
has visited the plant."

"Look Mum, the bee has gone right inside
that flower," said Sam.

"Yes, he will drink the nectar at the bottom
of the flower," Mum said. "Then when his legs
are heavy with pollen and he has drunk enough
nectar from the flowers, he will fly back to
the hive."

"There he goes," said Sam. "He's gone into
the hive."

"What do the bees do in the hive?" said Sam.

"They look after the queen bee and they make honey from the nectar," said Mum.

"And in the house we can eat the honey," said Sam. "I'm hungry."

So Mum and Sam went inside and Mum made honey sandwiches for tea.